武満 徹

混声合唱のための

うた Ⅰ

TORU TAKEMITSU
SONGS Ⅰ

for mixed chorus

SJ 1070

SCHOTT

混声合唱のための『うた I 』に収録されている《小さな空》、《うたうだけ》、《小さな部屋で》、《恋のかくれんぼ》、《見えないこども》、以上 5 曲は、作曲者自身により、東京混声合唱団のために合唱に編曲されたものである。また、《明日ハ晴レカナ、曇リカナ》は晋友会合唱団のＣＤ録音を機に作曲された。

初演と演奏時間：

《小さな空》──1981年 4 月21日、東京。田中信昭指揮東京混声合唱団。約 5 分。

《うたうだけ》──1981年 7 月 1 日、東京。田中信昭指揮東京混声合唱団。約4.5分。

《小さな部屋で》──1981年12月 3 日、東京。田中信昭指揮東京混声合唱団。約 4 分。

《恋のかくれんぼ》──1982年 4 月19日、東京。田中信昭指揮東京混声合唱団。約 2 分。

《見えないこども》──1982年 6 月28日、東京。田中信昭指揮東京混声合唱団。約3.5分。

《明日ハ晴レカナ、曇リカナ》──1992年 9 月15日、川口。関屋晋指揮晋友会。約 2 分。

Five pieces of this album "Songs I," — *Chiisana Sora (Small Sky)*, *Utau dake (I Just Sing)*, *Chiisana Heya de (In a Small Room)*, *Koi no Kakurembo (The Game of Love)* and *Mienai Kodomo (Unseen Child)* — were arranged for chorus by the composer from his original solo songs for the Tokyo Philharmonic Chorus, and *Ashita wa Hare kana, Kumori kana (Will Tomorrow, I Wonder, Be Cloudy or Clear?)* was composed for Shin-yu Kai Choir on the occasion of their CD recording.

First performance and the duration of each song:

Chiisana Sora (Small Sky) —— April 21, 1981 in Tokyo by the Tokyo Philharmonic Chorus conducted by Nobuaki Tanaka. About 5 minutes.
Utau dake (I Just Sing) —— July 1, 1981 in Tokyo by the Tokyo Philharmonic Chorus conducted by Nobuaki Tanaka. About 4.5 minutes.
Chiisana Heya de (In a Small Room) —— December 3, 1981 in Tokyo by the Tokyo Philharmonic Chorus conducted by Nobuaki Tanaka. About 4 minutes.
Koi no Kakurembo (The Game of Love) —— April 19, 1982 in Tokyo by the Tokyo Philharmonic Chorus conducted by Nobuaki Tanaka. About 2 minutes.
Mienai Kodomo (Unseen Child) —— June 28, 1982 in Tokyo by the Tokyo Philharmonic Chorus conducted by Nobuaki Tanaka. About 3.5 minutes.
Ashita wa Hare kana, Kumori kana (Will Tomorrow, I Wonder, Be Cloudy or Clear?) —— September 15, 1992 in Kawaguchi by Shin-yu Kai Choir conducted by Shin Sekiya. About 2 minutes.

目次

小さな空（武満徹　詞）——————5

うたうだけ（谷川俊太郎　詞）——————11

小さな部屋で（川路明　詞）——————14

恋のかくれんぼ（谷川俊太郎　詞）——————18

見えないこども（谷川俊太郎　詞）——————21

明日ハ晴レカナ、曇リカナ（武満徹　詞）——————24

Contents

Chiisana Sora (Small Sky)
Words by Toru Takemitsu——————5

Utau dake (I Just Sing)
Words by Shuntaro Tanikawa——————11

Chiisana Heya de (In a Small Room)
Words by Akira Kawaji——————14

Koi no Kakurembo (The Game of Love)
Words by Shuntaro Tanikawa——————18

Mienai Kodomo (Unseen Child)
Words by Shuntaro Tanikawa——————21

Ashita wa Hare kana, Kumori kana (Will Tomorrow, I Wonder, Be Cloudy or Clear?)
Words by Toru Takemitsu——————24

小さな空
Chiisana Sora (Small Sky)

武満 徹 詞・曲
Words and Music by Toru Takemitsu

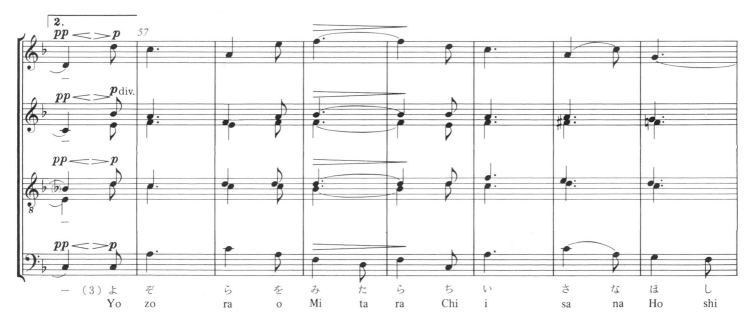

が な み だ の よ ー に ひ か ー っ て い た
ga Na mi da no yo - ni Hi ka - tte i ta

い た ず ら が す ぎ て し か ら れ て な い
I ta zu ra ga Su gi te Shi ka ra re te Na i

rall. _ _ //   poco rall. _ _ //   rall. _ _ _ _ _ //

こ ど も の こ ろ を お も い だ し た ー
Ko do mo no Ko ro o O mo i da shi ta -

こ ど ー も の こ ろ を お も い だ し た ー
Ko do - - mo no Ko ro o O mo i da shi ta -

た こ ど も ー の こ ろ を ー お も い だ し た ー
ta Ko do mo - no Ko ro o - O mo i da shi ta -

こ ど も の こ ろ を ー お も い だ し た ー
Ko do mo no Ko ro o - O mo i da shi ta

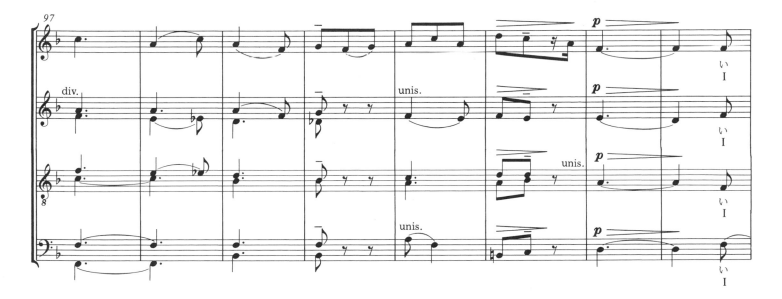

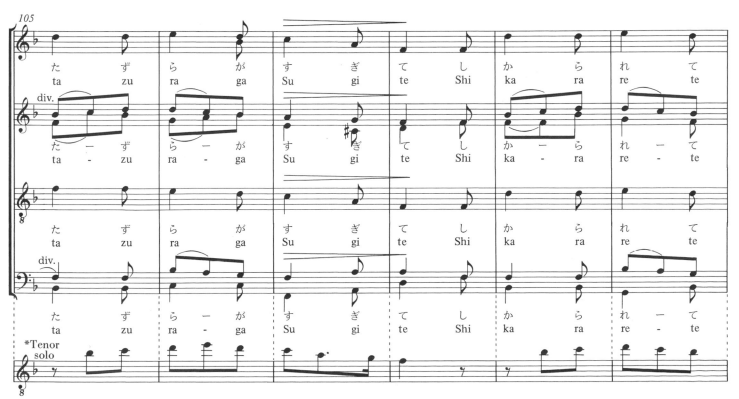

＊この tenor solo は falsetto がのぞましい。口笛でもよい。
即興的な気分でオブリガートする。(もちろん歌詞はうたわない。)

＊For this tenor solo falsetto is preferable but whistling is acceptable.
Obbligato in an improvisation (without words).

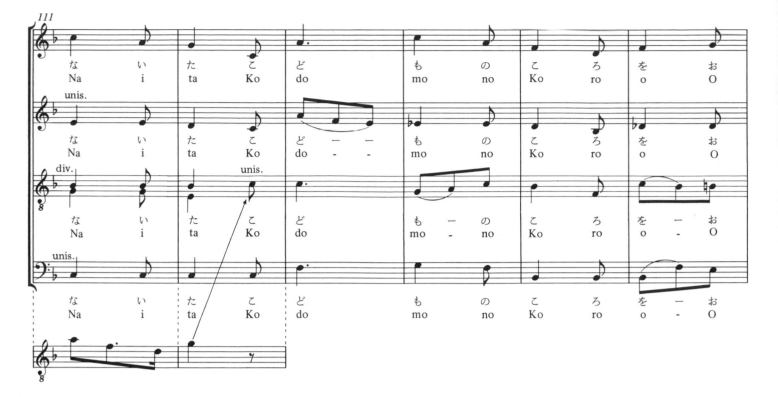

うたうだけ

Utau dake (I Just Sing)

谷川俊太郎　詞
武満 徹　曲
Words by Shuntaro Tanikawa
Music by Toru Takemitsu

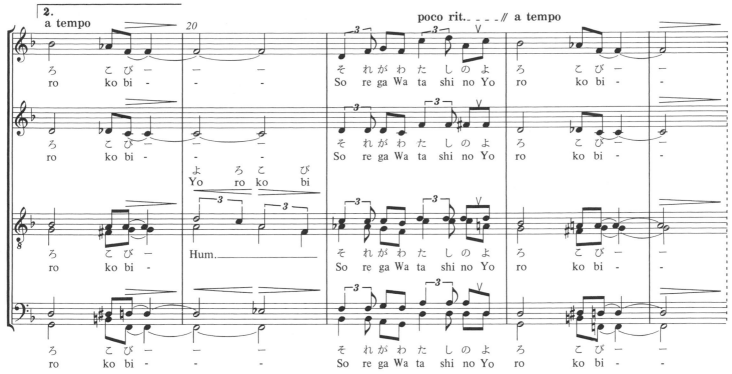

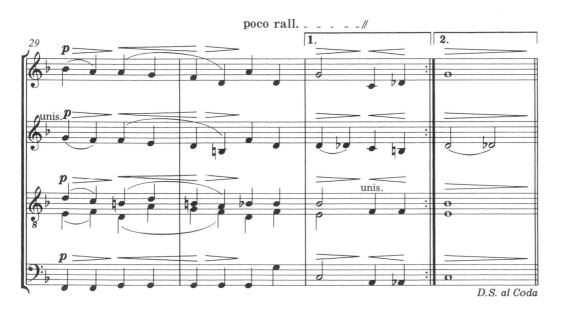

小さな部屋で

Chiisana Heya de (In a Small Room)

川路 明 詞
武満 徹 曲
Words by Akira Kawaji
Music by Toru Takemitsu

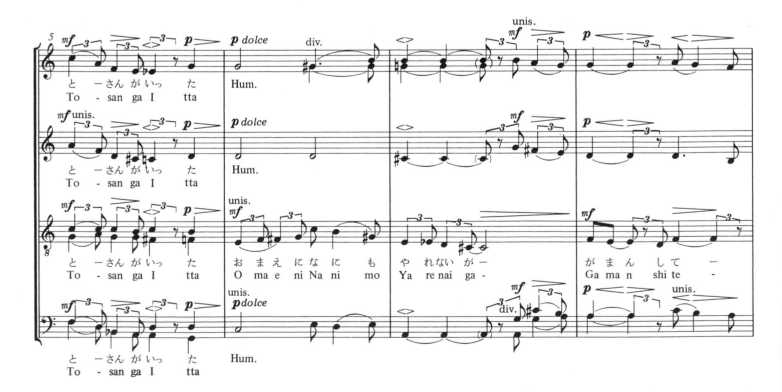

恋のかくれんぼ
Koi no Kakurembo (The Game of Love)

谷川俊太郎　詞
武満　徹　曲
Words by Shuntaro Tanikawa
Music by Toru Takemitsu

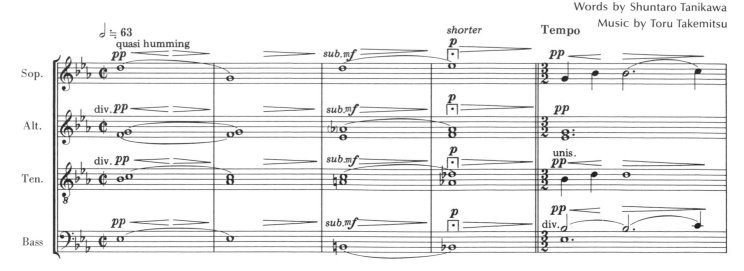

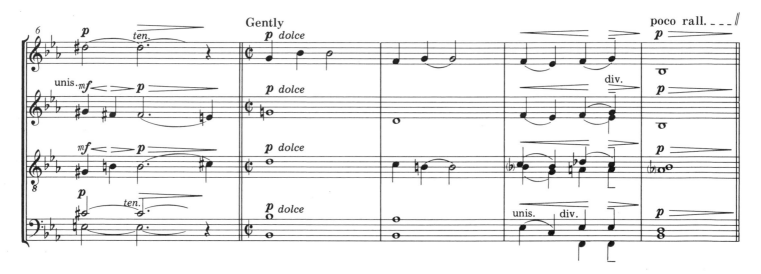

見えないこども
Mienai Kodomo (Unseen Child)

谷川俊太郎　詞
武満　徹　曲

Words by Shuntaro Tanikawa
Music by Toru Takemitsu

22

明日ハ晴レカナ、曇リカナ

Ashita wa Hare kana, Kumori kana

(Will Tomorrow, I Wonder, Be Cloudy or Clear?)

武満 徹 詞・曲
Words and Music by Toru Takemitsu

武満 徹

混声合唱のための

うた Ⅰ

小さな空

武満 徹 詞

1　青空みたら
　綿のような雲が
　悲しみをのせて
　飛んでいった
　（リフレイン）
　　　いたずらが過ぎて
　　　叱かられて泣いた
　　　こどもの頃を憶いだした

2　夕空みたら
　教会の窓の
　ステンドグラスが
　眞赫に燃えてた

3　夜空をみたら
　小さな星が
　涙のように
　光っていた

うたうだけ

谷川俊太郎　詞

1　むずかしいことばは
　いらないの
　かなしいときには
　うたうだけ
　うたうと、うたうと、うたうと
　かなしみはふくれる
　ふうせんのように
　それが　わたしの　よろこび

2　なぐさめのことばは
　いらないの
　かなしいときには
　うたうだけ
　うたうと、うたうと、うたうと
　かなしみはふくれる
　ふうせんのように
　それが　わたしの　よろこび

小さな部屋で

川路　明　詞

1　小さな部屋で
　父さんが言った
　おまえに何もやれないが
　がまんして、がまんして
　おまえの胸は若いんだから
　（リフレイン）
　　　春がきたけど
　　　なにもない
　　　夏がきたけど
　　　なにもない
　　　何もないけど暖い
　　　あたたかいのは空と風
　　　あたたかいのは雲と陽光
　　　ああ、ひとのこころの暖ければ
　　　何もないけど
　　　それこそすべて

2　小さな部屋で
　母さんが言った
　おまえに何もやれないが
　がまんして、がまんして
　垣根に花がいっぱいだから

恋のかくれんぼ

谷川俊太郎　詞

1　まあるい地球に朝がきて
　だれかとだれかが
　かくれんぼ
　もおいいかい
　まだだよ
　かくれるだれかの耳朵に
　みつけるだれかがキッスしてる

2　まあるい地球に夜がきて
　わたしとあなたと
　通りゃんせ
　往きはよいよい
　帰りはこわい
　ここはどこの細道じゃ
　ふたりの恋の細道じゃ

見えないこども

谷川俊太郎　詞

1　まだ　生まれないこども
　誰かの　こども
　朝になると　笑ってる
　朝になると　窓の外で

2　まだ、実らない胡桃
　緑の　胡桃
　夜になると　揺れている
　夜になると　森のなかで

3　もう生まれないこども
　わたしの　こども
　朝になると　歌ってる
　朝になると　空を飛ぶ

明日ハ晴レカナ、曇リカナ

武満　徹　詞

1　昨日ノ悲シミ
　今日ノ涙
　明日ハ晴レカナ
　曇リカナ

2　昨日ノ苦シミ
　今日ノ悩ミ
　明日ハ晴レカナ
　曇リカナ

Toru Takemitsu
SONGS I

for mixed chorus

Chiisana Sora (Small Sky)

Words by Toru Takemitsu

1   I looked up at the blue sky.
    Clouds like cotton wool
    flew by
    carrying sorrow.

    (Refrain)
    I recalled my childhood
    when I was scolded for my mischief
    and I cried.

2   I looked up at the evening sky.
    Stained glass windows
    in a church
    burned deep red.

3   I looked up at the night sky.
    A tiny star
    glimmered
    like a tear drop.

Utau dake (I Just Sing)

Words by Shuntaro Tanikawa

1   When I feel sad and have no use for troubling words,
    I just sing.
    If I sing, if I sing, if I sing,
    My sadness blows up like a balloon
    and gives me joy.

2   When I feel sad and have no use for comforting words,
    I just sing.
    If I sing, if I sing, if I sing,
    My sadness blows up like a balloon
    and gives me joy.

Chiisana Heya de (In a Small Room)

Words by Akira Kawaji

1 In a small room, my father spoke:
"There is nothing I can give you," he said,
"but be patient, be patient,
for you are still young."

(Refrain)
Spring came, but there was nothing,
Summer came, but there was nothing.
There wasn't a thing but it was warm.
Warm was the sky, the wind,
Warm were the clouds and sunlight.
Oh, if only people's hearts were warm!
Though it were nothing, it would be everything.

2 In a small room, my mother spoke:
"There is nothing I can give you," she said,
"But be patient, be patient,
for the hedge is full of flowers."

Koi no Kakurembo (The Game of Love)

Words by Shuntaro Tanikawa

1 Morning comes to the round, round Earth
And someone's playing hide-and-seek
With someone.
Ready or not, here I come!
Not yet! Not yet!
The one who finds the one who hides
Kisses the tip of his ear.

2 Night comes to the round, round Earth
And you and I are playing
"Please pass through."
Going out is lots of fun
But coming back is scary.
What narrow way is this?
It is the narrow way of love.

Note: The words "please pass through" refer to a
traditional children's game similar to "London
Bridge." When the children pass under the arch
in one direction, "going out," they are safe, but
when they turn around and pass through from
the other direction, "coming back," they may
well be caught. Lines 10-13 are taken from the
song the children sing while playing the game.
The question "What narrow way is this?" in the
children's song is answered, "It is the narrow
way of the heavenly gods."

Mienai Kodomo (Unseen Child)

Words by Shuntaro Tanikawa

1 The child not yet born
Somebody's child
When morning comes is laughing
When morning comes outside the window.

2 The walnut not yet ripe
Green walnut
When nighttime comes is trembling
When nighttime comes deep in the woods.

3 The child who will no longer be born
My child
When morning comes is singing
When morning comes she flies across the sky.

Ashita wa Hare kana, Kumori kana (Will Tomorrow, I Wonder, Be Cloudy or Clear?)

Words by Toru Takemitsu

1 Yesterday's sorrows
Today's tears
Will tomorrow, I wonder,
Be cloudy or clear?

2 Yesterday's troubles
Today's pain
Will tomorrow, I wonder,
Be cloudy or clear?

(English translation by Ella Louise Rutledge)

武満 徹《うた I》　　　　　　　　　　　●

混声合唱のための

初版発行─────────────────────1992年8月5日

第2版第13刷⑱────────────────2021年7月21日

発行─────────────────ショット・ミュージック株式会社

──────────────東京都千代田区内神田1-10-1 平富ビル3階

──────────────〒101-0047

──────────────(03)6695-2450

──────────────www.schottjapan.com

──────────────ISBN 978-4-89066-370-5

──────────────ISMN M-65001-107-5

現代の音楽
MUSIC OF OUR TIME

VOICE(S) / CHOIR

武満 徹 Toru Takemitsu (1930–1996)

うた I
Songs I
for mixed chorus
Text: Akira Kawaji, Shuntaro Tanikawa and the composer (in Japanese)
SJ 1070 . . . 1800 円

うた II
Songs II
for mixed chorus
Text: Kuniharu Akiyama, Mann Izawa, Shuntaro Tanikawa and the composer (in Japanese)
SJ 1081 . . . 1800 円

風の馬
Wind Horse
for mixed chorus
Words: Kuniharu Akiyama (in Japanese)
SJ 1082 . . . 1800 円

芝生
Grass
for male chorus
Text: Shuntaro Tanikawa (in English, translated by W. S. Merwin)
SJ 1009 . . . 800 円

手づくり諺 ——四つのポップ・ソング——
Handmade Proverbs —Four Pop Songs—
for six male voices
Text: Shuzo Takiguchi (in English, translated by Kenneth Lyons)
SJ 1041 . . . 1000 円

武満徹 SONGS （大竹伸朗・絵）
Toru Takemitsu: Songs
20 songs composed by Toru Takemitsu.
Artwork by Shinro Ohtake.

Melody with piano arrangement and chord names.

17 Japanese language lyrics in original Japanese characters and phoneticized by Roman alphabets.
English text adapted by Ella Louise Rutledge & Kirsti Kaldro.

3 songs originally written in German, French and Spanish.

SJ 2000 . . . 5000 円

MI·YO·TA
MI·YO·TA
for mixed chorus (arrangement by Ryusuke Numajiri)
Text: Shuntaro Tanikawa (in Japanese)
SJ 1190 . . . 500 円

湯浅譲二 Joji Yuasa (1929–)

天気予報所見
Observations on Weather Forecasts
for Baritone and trumpet . . . SJ 1029 . . . 1200 円

声のための「音楽」（オトガク）
Phonomatopoeia
for mixed voices . . . SJ 1128 . . . 2000 円

一柳 慧 Toshi Ichiyanagi (1933–)

詩の中の風景 I
Scenes of Poems I
for mixed chorus and violoncello
Text: Rin Ishigaki, Shinkichi Ito, Mitsuharu Kaneko and Hiroshi Osada (in Japanese)
SJ 1119 . . . 3200 円

細川俊夫 Toshio Hosokawa (1955–)

アヴェ・マリア
Ave Maria
for mixed chorus . . . SJ 1065 . . . 2800 円

アヴェ・マリス・ステッラ
Ave Maris Stella
for mixed chorus . . . SJ 1088 . . . 3200 円

恋歌 I
Renka I
for Soprano and guitar
Text from Manyoshu and Shin-Kokinshu (in Japanese)
SJ 1066 . . . 1400 円

歌う木 ——武満 徹へのレクイエム——
Singing Trees —Requiem for Toru Takemitsu—
for children's chorus
Text: the composer (in Japanese)
SJ 1113 . . . 2000 円

鈴木優人 Masato Suzuki (1981–)

アポカリプシス ii
Apokalypsis ii
for vocal ensemble
Text from the Vulgate, "Revelation of John" 6:1-17 and 8:1
SJ 1209 . . . 2700 円

ショット・ミュージック株式会社
東京都千代田区内神田1-10-1　平富ビル3階　〒101-0047
電話 (03) 6695-2450　ファクス (03) 6695-2579
sales@schottjapan.com　www.schottjapan.com

SCHOTT MUSIC CO. LTD.
Hiratomi Bldg., 1-10-1 Uchikanda, Chiyoda-ku, Tokyo 101-0047
Telephone: (+81)3-6695-2450 Fax: (+81)3-6695-2579
sales@schottjapan.com　www.schottjapan.com

（価格には消費税が含まれておりません。）